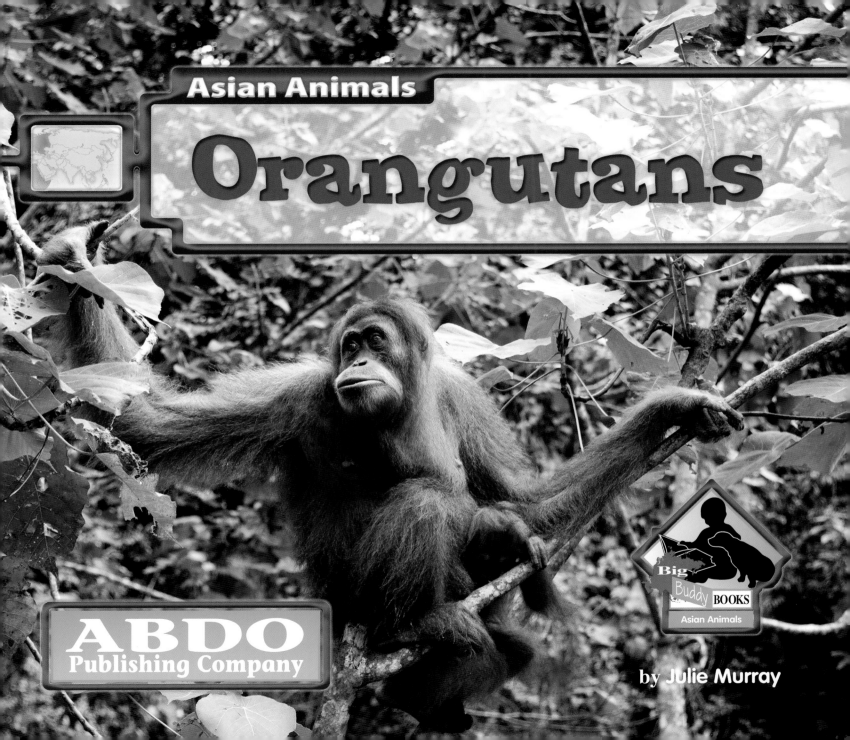

Asian Animals

Orangutans

ABDO
Publishing Company

Big Buddy BOOKS
Asian Animals

by Julie Murray

VISIT US AT
www.abdopublishing.com

Published by ABDO Publishing Company, PO Box 398166, Minneapolis, Minnesota 55439.

Printed in the United States of America, North Mankato, Minnesota.
082012
012013

♻ PRINTED ON RECYCLED PAPER

Coordinating Series Editor: Rochelle Baltzer
Editor: Marcia Zappa
Contributing Editors: Megan M. Gunderson, Grace Hansen, Sarah Tieck
Graphic Design: Maria Hosley
Cover Photograph: *Shutterstock*: Matej Hudovernik.
Interior Photographs/Illustrations: *Animals Animals-Earth Scenes*: Arden/Marent, Thomas (p. 11), Shah, Anup (p. 27); *Fotosearch.com*: ©SURZ (pp. 5, 8); *Getty Images*: Rodney Brindamour/National Geographic (p. 20), Timothy Laman/National Geographic (p. 17); *Glow Images*: Juniors Bildarchiv/Juniors (p. 25); *iStockphoto*: ©iStockphoto.com/HU-JUN (p. 4), ©iStockphoto.com/Mac99 (p. 9), ©iStockphoto.com/phleum (p. 9); *Minden Pictures*: Neil Lucas/npl (p. 23); *Photo Researchers, Inc.*: Alain Compost (p. 21); *Shutterstock*: Eric Gevaert (p. 29), Warren Goldwain (p. 9), Mau Horna (p. 23), Image Focus (p. 4), Nathape (p. 19), Uryadnikov Sergey (pp. 7, 13, 15, 17).

Library of Congress Cataloging-in-Publication Data

Murray, Julie, 1969-
  Orangutans / Julie Murray.
    p. cm. -- (Asian animals)
  ISBN 978-1-61783-556-8
  1. Orangutan--Juvenile literature. I. Title.
  QL737.P96M8736 2013
  599.88'3--dc23
                                    2012023974

Contents

Long ago, nearly all land on Earth was one big mass. About 200 million years ago, the land began to break into **continents**. One of these continents is Asia.

Orangutans are a type of ape. They are known for their intelligence, large size, and reddish-brown fur.

Asia is the largest **continent**. It includes many countries and **cultures**. It also has different types of land and interesting animals. One of these animals is the orangutan. In the wild, orangutans are only found in Asia.

Orangutan Territory

There are two types of orangutans. The Bornean orangutan is found on the Southeast Asian island of Borneo. The Sumatran orangutan is found on the Southeast Asian island of Sumatra.

On these islands, orangutans live in forests. Usually, the forests are warm and wet. But sometimes, they are drier.

Borneo

Sumatra

 Orangutan Territory

Orangutans are one of the five main types of apes. The others are bonobos, chimpanzees, gibbons, and gorillas.

Uncovered!

Borneo is the third-largest island in the world. It is split between the countries of Brunei, Malaysia, and Indonesia. Sumatra is the sixth-largest island in the world. It is part of Indonesia.

Welcome to Asia!

If you took a trip to where orangutans live, you might find…

…many cultures.

Sumatra and Borneo are home to many different groups of people. These include the Acehnese, Batak, Malay, Minangkabau, Kadazans, Dayak, and Chinese. These groups have their own cultures and languages. *Orangutan* is a Malay word. It means "person of the forest."

...giant flowers.

Two of the world's largest flowers grow on Sumatra. These are the titan arum (*right*) and the rafflesia. The titan arum is also unusual because it smells like rotting meat!

...monsoons.

The weather on Sumatra and Borneo is controlled by the Asian monsoon. A monsoon is a wind that changes with the seasons. Monsoons often cause heavy rains and floods during certain times of the year. On Sumatra and Borneo, rain is heaviest in December, January, and February.

...lots of people.

Orangutans generally avoid people. Yet, many live in the heavily-populated country of Indonesia. With more than 240 million people, the country has the fourth-largest population in the world!

Take a Closer Look

Orangutans have rounded bodies, short legs, and long arms. An orangutan's oval face has two deep-set eyes. It also has a large **snout** with a small nose and thin mouth.

Orangutans have **shaggy** fur on their bodies and heads. Dark skin covers their faces and the bottoms of their hands and feet.

A male orangutan's arm span may reach seven to eight feet (2.1 to 2.4 m). When standing, his hands almost touch the ground!

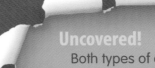

Grown Men

There are two types of adult male orangutans. These are unflanged and flanged. Unflanged males look like adult females. Flanged males look different. They have large neck pouches under their chins. And, they have wide cheek pads. Some unflanged males become flanged.

Flanged males are very large. They stand four to five feet (1.2 to 1.5 m) tall. And, they weigh 100 to 300 pounds (45 to 136 kg). Unflanged males and adult females weigh about half as much.

A flanged orangutan's cheek pads and neck pouch are covered in rough, dark skin.

Flanged male orangutans do not get along well. They usually avoid one another. But sometimes, they fight over females.

When two flanged males fight, they run forward and grab each other. Then, they bite each other's heads and cheek pads. A fight may last a few minutes to more than an hour!

Scientists don't understand when, why, or how unflanged males become flanged. Some believe that only one flanged male can live in a range at a time.

Uncovered!

Flanged males use their neck pouches to make loud calls. Sometimes, the calls can be heard almost one mile (1.6 km) away! They get the attention of females and help keep other males away.

Life in Trees

Orangutans spend almost their whole lives in trees. They sleep in nests built out of branches and leaves. Sometimes, they use large leaves as roofs. This helps keep them dry when it rains.

Orangutans move from tree to tree by swinging on branches. Sometimes, they can't find a strong branch to carry them. Then, they come down to the ground and walk. But, they usually don't do this unless they have to.

Uncovered!

Sumatran orangutans almost never come down from the trees. It is more common for Bornean orangutans to do this. On the ground, orangutans walk on all fours.

Orangutans generally live alone. But, groups of females and teenagers sometimes live near one another. And, females live closely with their young.

Orangutans usually build a new nest each night. Sometimes, they also build nests during the day to nap in.

Orangutans are well built for living in trees. Their arms and hands are very strong. This helps them hold up their large bodies while swinging from branch to branch.

An orangutan's long arms also help it reach faraway branches. And its long, curved hands and feet help it hold on tightly.

Orangutans are the largest animals in the world that live in trees.

19

Sharp Minds

Orangutans are known for being smart. They often make and use tools. They use sticks to scratch themselves, guard against stinging bugs, and collect food. And, they use large leaves as ponchos and umbrellas.

Like humans, orangutans have opposable thumbs that move freely of their other fingers. This makes it easy for them to hold things such as tools.

Orangutans use sticks to catch fish. They also use them to collect insects and honey. And, they use them to pull in fruit that is too far to reach.

Mealtime

Orangutans eat many different foods found in their treetop homes. More than half of what they eat is fruit. Their favorites include figs and durians.

Orangutans also eat leaves, bark, flowers, and nuts. Sometimes they eat honey, eggs, and bugs. And every once in a while, they eat a type of small animal called a slow loris.

Durians are often called the "king of fruits." Their outsides are covered in sharp spikes. But, the fruit inside is soft. Many people think durians smell bad but taste good.

Baby Orangutans

Orangutans are **mammals**. Female orangutans usually have one baby every six to nine years. At birth, an orangutan baby weighs about three and a half pounds (1.6 kg). For food, it drinks its mother's milk.

Uncovered!

Young orangutans have predators. Leopards and pythons hunt Bornean orangutans. Tigers hunt Sumatran orangutans.

At first, an orangutan baby rides on its mother's belly, side, or back. After a few years, it follows her through the treetops.

Young orangutans are very close with their mothers. Mothers teach them where to find food, how to eat it, and how to build nests. Young orangutans stay with their mothers for 6 to 12 years.

Uncovered!

Sometimes, a young orangutan comes to a gap between trees too wide for it to cross. So, its mother reaches across and acts as a bridge for her young to crawl over.

Young orangutans are known to be smart and curious.

Survivors

Life in Asia isn't easy for orangutans. People cut down trees in their **habitats** for lumber and to make farms and roads. They also kill orangutans for their meat. And, people capture them to sell as pets.

Still, orangutans **survive**. There are laws against killing them. But, more needs to be done to keep them from dying out. Orangutans help make Asia an amazing place!

In the wild, orangutans live for 30 to 40 years.

Wow!
I'll bet you never knew...

...that orangutans can bend easily. Humans have a tight band that connects their legs to their bodies. Orangutans do not. So, they can move their legs more freely.

...that orangutans have talented toes! Their big toes are opposable, like thumbs. So, they can easily hold objects with their feet.

...that certain groups of orangutans use leaves as napkins. This practice is learned from other group members. It isn't known by orangutans outside the group.

Important Words

continent one of Earth's seven main land areas.

culture (KUHL-chuhr) the arts, beliefs, and ways of life of a group of people.

habitat a place where a living thing is naturally found.

mammal a member of a group of living beings. Mammals make milk to feed their babies and usually have hair or fur on their skin.

shaggy made up of long, tangled hair or fur.

snout a part of the face, including the nose and the mouth, that sticks out. Some animals, such as orangutans, have a snout.

survive to continue to live or exist.

Web Sites

To learn more about orangutans, visit ABDO Publishing Company online. Web sites about orangutans are featured on our Book Links page. These links are routinely monitored and updated to provide the most current information available.

www.abdopublishing.com

Index